START-UP HISTORY

Homes

Stewart Ross

W
FRANKLIN WATTS
LONDON • SYDNEY

This edition published in 2023 by Hodder & Stoughton

Copyright © White-Thomson Publishing 2014

All rights reserved.

Produced for Franklin Watts by
White-Thomson Publishing Ltd

www.wtpub.co.uk
+44 (0) 843 208 7460

Editor: Anna Lee
Consultant: Nora Granger
Designer: Tessa Barwick

This book was first published by Evans Brothers Ltd. It has been revised and fully updated in line with the KS1 history curriculum.

A CIP catalogue record for this book is available from the British Library.

Dewey no: 643'.09
Hardback ISBN: 978 1 4451 3502 1
Paperback ISBN: 978 1 4451 3504 5
Library eBook ISBN: 978 1 4451 3503 8

Printed in the United Kingdom

Franklin Watts
An imprint of Hachette Children's Books,
Part of Hodder & Stoughton,
Carmelite House
50 Victoria Embankment
London, EC4Y 0DZ

www.hachettechildrens.co.uk

Picture Acknowledgements: Beamish The Living Museum of the North: 19r; Bridgeman 21; Chris Dorney/Shutterstock: 4t; Chris Fairclough: 5r, 6b, 7b; Shutterstock: 4b, 6t, 7t, 15r, 16-17dps, 20; Thinkstock: cover t, cover b; York Museums Trust (York Castle Museum): 8-9dps, 10, 11t, 11b, 12-13dps, 14, 15l, 18, 19l, cover main; Zul Mukhida: 5l

Every effort has been made to clear copyright. Should there be any inadvertent omission, please apply to the publisher for rectification.

Every effort has been made by the Publishers to ensure that the websites in this book are suitable for children, that they are of the highest educational value and that they contain no inappropriate or offensive material. However, because of the nature of the Internet, it is impossible to guarantee that the contents of these sites will not be altered. We strongly advise that Internet access is supervised by a responsible adult.

Contents

Different houses 4

Roofs and windows 6

Inside a Victorian house 8

Fireplaces 10

A kitchen from the past 12

Changing cookers 14

A modern bathroom 16

Toilets inside and outside 18

Which is older? 20

Further information for Parents and Teachers 22

Index 24

Different houses

▼ This is a **bungalow**.
It was **built** about 20 **years ago**.

▲ This is a block of **flats**.
It is about 40 years **old**.

4 bungalow built years ago flats

▼ This **house** was built about 90 years ago.

▲ This **terraced** house is more than 110 years old. It is **Victorian**.

old   terraced   house   Victorian

5

Roofs and windows

◀ Here is the roof of the bungalow. It has clay tiles.

▶ The roof of the terraced house has slate tiles. It has many chimneys.

6   roof   clay   tiles   slate   chimneys

◀ The bungalow has **plastic window frames**.

▶ The terraced house has **sash** windows. The frames are made of **wood**. How do they open?

plastic window frames sash wood

Inside a Victorian house

This is a living room from Victorian times.

The **mantelpiece** is over the **fireplace**.

What can you see on the mantelpiece?

mantelpiece   fireplace   pictures

There are many **pictures** on the walls.

The floor is covered with a **rug**. Underneath the rug are **floorboards**.

How is this living room different from your living room at **home**?

rug   floorboards   home

9

Fireplaces

Here is the Victorian fireplace.
The coal scuttle and tongs are next to the fire.
What are the tongs for?

coal scuttle   tongs

▲ This fire is in a house that is 60 years old. It uses **electricity**.

▶ This **modern** fire uses **gas**. but looks as if it **burns** wood.

electricity   modern   gas   burns

A kitchen from the past

This is a **kitchen** from about 70 years ago.

How is the **sink** different from the sink in your kitchen?

12   kitchen   sink

There is a **pressure cooker** on the **stove**.

The **kettle** is also on the stove.
Most modern kitchens have electric kettles.

How else is this kitchen different from a modern one?

pressure cooker   **stove**   **kettle**

Changing cookers

This Victorian **cooker** was called a **'range'**.

It burned wood or **coal**.

Food cooked slowly in the **oven** beside the fire.

14

cooker   range   coal

▼ This is an electric cooker from 60 years ago.

How is it the same as a modern cooker? How is it different?

▲ This modern microwave uses electricity. It cooks food very quickly.

oven   microwave

A modern bathroom

▶ This **bathroom** has a **basin**, a **bath** and a **toilet**.

What else can you see that belongs in a bathroom?

16 bathroom   basin   bath   toilet

◀ There is a shower over the bath.

In the past, many homes didn't have bathrooms.

People washed in a tin bathtub in the kitchen or the living room.

shower   past   tin   bathtub

Toilets inside and outside

Here is the toilet in a modern bathroom.

The **seat** and **lid** are made from plastic.

18

seat　　lid　　flushed

◀ This toilet is from about 70 years ago.
It was **flushed** by pulling the **handle** on the end of the **chain**.

▲ One hundred years ago most toilets were like this one. They were found **outside** the house.

handle   chain   outside

Which is older?

One of these bedrooms is modern and one is Victorian. Can you tell which is which?

Look carefully at the beds, the furniture and the decoration.

20

bedrooms   beds

**The bedroom on the left is modern.
The one on the right is from Victorian times.**

furniture   decoration   **21**

Further information for

New history and homes words highlighted in the text:

ago	clay	gas	oven	slate
basin	coal	handle	past	stove
bath	coal scuttle	home	pictures	terraced
bathroom	cooker	house	plastic	tiles
bathtub	decoration	kettle	pressure cooker	tin
bedrooms	electricity	kitchen	range	toilet
beds	fireplace	lid	roof	tongs
built	flats	mantelpiece	rug	Victorian
bungalow	floorboards	microwave	sash	window
burns	flushed	modern	seat	wood
chain	frames	old	shower	years
chimneys	furniture	outside	sink	

Background Information

CHRONOLOGY OF SELECTED BACKGROUND INFORMATION

1890s   Electric light in homes of the well-off. Bulk of the population living in sub-standard housing without gas, electricity, bathroom or inside lavatory.

1900   First electric cookers appearing. Gas cookers widespread in wealthy homes.

1907   First electric washing machine.

1919-24   Increased subsidies for council housing.

1919-39   2.5 million private homes built. Average price of a 'semi' £450.

1935   12% of the population living in overcrowded conditions (two or more per room).

1936   17.8% of the population of York unable to afford adequate food, housing, heating and lighting.

1939   90% of homes heated by open fires. 66% homes wired for electricity.

1947   Green belts introduced around large cities.

1948   Microwave oven invented.

1951   33% of British homes without a plumbed bath.

1954   Transistor radios available.

1956   22.5% of Scottish homes overcrowded.

1960s   St Anne's district of Nottingham: 91% of homes with outside lavatory; 85% without bathrooms, 54% without a hot water system.

Parents and Teachers

1970s Fitted carpets and use of showers (rather than baths) becoming widespread.

1980s Home ownership growing rapidly.

1990s Housing shortage owing to swiftly growing number of households.

2000s Houses become greener with doorstep recycling collection, solar panels and triple glazing.

2008 Worldwide credit crunch damages housing market.

2010s Multigenerational homes become common again as house prices increase.

2013 Over 90% of households have internet access.

Possible Activities:

Visit to nearby homes of different periods.

Draw features of homes from different periods.

Make a frieze timeline.

Work out how people lived from the objects that surrounded them – e.g. the amount of time needed to clean a range meant that it either stayed dirty or someone spent a long time each week cleaning it. Who?

Make a 'home corner' of different rooms and periods.

Invite adults in to talk about their homes at some specific time in the past.

Some Topics for Discussion:

Differences between homes of the same period – e.g. Victorian mansion and slum.

Role of servants before labour-saving devices.

Health and the spread of bathrooms and flushing toilets.

Safety in the home – open fires, etc.

Changing design and materials for household objects.

Further Information

BOOKS
FOR CHILDREN

Houses Long Ago (See Inside) by Rob Lloyd Jones and Barry Ablett (Usborne, 2010)

Project Geography: Homes by Sally Hewitt (Franklin Watts, 2013)

Where You Live: Houses and Homes by Ruth Nason (Franklin Watts, 2010)

Your Local Area: Homes by Ruth Thomson (Wayland, 2012)

FOR ADULTS

At Home: A Short History of Private Life by Bill Bryson (Black Swan, 2011)

If Walls Could Talk: An Intimate History of the Home by Lucy Worsley (Faber & Faber, 2012)

The Great Indoors: At Home in the Modern British House by Ben Highmore (Profile Books, 2014)

WEBSITES

www.bbc.co.uk/scotland/education/wwww/homes/kids/index_choice.shtml

www.geffrye-museum.org.uk/kidszone

history.parkfieldict.co.uk/modern1950s/1950s-homes

www.primaryhomeworkhelp.co.uk/houses.html

PLACES TO VISIT

The Geffrye Museum, London

Victoria and Albert Museum, London

York Castle Museum

Index

b
basin 16
bath 16, 17
bathrooms 16-17
bathtub 17
bedrooms 20-21
beds 20
bungalow 4, 6, 7

c
chimneys 6
coal 14
coal scuttle 10
cookers 14-15
   electric 15
   microwave 15
   pressure cooker 13
   range 14

f
fireplaces 8, 10-11
fire 14
   electric 11
   gas 11
   wood 10, 14
flats 4
floor 9
floorboards 9

k
kettle 13
kitchen 12-13, 17

l
living room 8-9, 17

m
mantelpiece 8
microwave 15

o
oven 14-15

p
pictures 8, 9

r
roofs 6
   clay tiles 6
   slate tiles 6
rug 9

s
shower 17
sink 12
stove 13

t
terraced house 5, 6, 7
toilets 16, 18-19
tongs 10

v
Victorian 5, 8, 10, 14, 20, 21

w
windows
  frames 7
  sash 7